William P. Swartz

Is the Bible Trustworthy?

William P. Swartz

Is the Bible Trustworthy?

ISBN/EAN: 9783337371128

Printed in Europe, USA, Canada, Australia, Japan

Cover: Foto ©Lupo / pixelio.de

More available books at **www.hansebooks.com**

Is the Bible

Trustworthy?

FIVE PAPERS BY

THE REV. WM. P. SWARTZ,

Pastor of Central Presbyterian Church,

WILMINGTON, DEL.

Porter & Co., Booksellers and Stationers,

409 Market Street, Wilmington, Del.

PREFACE.

These papers were originally addresses prepared in response to the interest of the writer's people in the current discussion of the Trustworthiness of the Bible. They were received with such favor and so many requests were made for their publication, that they were put in print as delivered. These separate parts are now gathered under one cover for the convenience of those wishing the papers in a form more easily handled and preserved. No attempt has been made to disguise the evidences of their first character; nor is there given any list of the works consulted, but an acknowledgment of obligation to many authors other than those named in the body of the work is freely made.

That they are adapted to the wants of many busy people, who ask what is the effect of all the discussion and of modern discoveries upon the accuracy and trustworthiness of the Bible, a number have freely testified. It is a matter of gratitude that God has already used them to win some wavering souls to unquestioning faith. That He may still further bless these words in commanding and confirming faith in His everlasting Word is the earnest prayer of   '   W. P. S.

Wilmington, Del., March, 1892.

CONTENTS.

Is the Bible Trustworthy?

BY THE REV. WILLIAM P. SWARTZ.

✣ PART I. ✣

"THY WORD IS TRUTH." John xvii:17.

THE QUESTION STATED.

Such is Christ's declaration concerning God's word. But is it true? is the question of many in our day. "One period," says a German writer, "has contended for his sepulchre, another for his body and blood, the present period contends for his word." And it is true, that every period of the church's history has been determined as much by the foes which it has confronted, as by its own internal development. The vitality of Christianity, its power to resist attack, triumphing the more it is opposed, are strong evidence of its divine origin, and its no less divine preservation. First came the age of persecutions, when believers endured the power of angry mobs, or the more terrible persecutions of the empire, always attesting, however, the presence of a living faith. Then it was that the church was made glorious in the triumphant martyrdom of a Fortuna, and a Blandina, of a Polycarp, of Justin, the Martyr, of Paeon, of Liberianus, and untold others, who cast the fear of death from them as the sunshine hurls the darkness from its path. Then followed a period of internal strife, when heresy after heresy threatened to vitiate both the truth and the faith which the church had received from the fathers. And the names of Athanasius and of Augustine, defenders of the revealed truth of God's word, became conspicuous. Then followed the age of corruption, when the purity of the faith was covered with a veneering of superstition and error, until the mighty Luther, with heroic zeal, hammered off this overlaying corruption as he nailed the 95 theses to the door of the electoral church at Wittenberg. The Reformation began almost at the same time as the revival of learning. The light of a pure gospel and of an unchained Bible had hardly begun to shine with uninterrupted ray, when many, proud of their recent acquisitions of knowledge, began to hurl the weapons of their intellects at this system, whose keystone is faith. Then followed in quick succession the assaults of the atheists, which were met by William Paley in works which are still classical; and a little later the deists hurled themselves against the light of this word, but the answer of Bishop Butler was itself unanswerable. During all these centuries the disciples of Christ have contended for some truth which they have received from their Divine Master. But now they are called to defend the citadel itself, to maintain the integrity and authority of God's word. Never was the contest more hotly, or more skillfully waged by our foes without; never have more aid and comfort been given to these foes of the Bible, than is now afforded by the weakness and shifting of some of its professed friends. We need not be much disturbed by the higher criticism, for its results, while dogmatic enough to deceive the wavering, can have only the authority of a critic's opinion. There is little or no historical evidence for its positions, nor any fact of nature which can give its results permanency. In its spirit of deeper, reverent, yet independent, study of the word of God there is probably more of help than of hurt.

There is, however, presented to us a more serious challenge. It is the challenge of students who claim to have

2

found in the Bible errors which must have been in the original manuscripts; errors, which it must be acknowledged are due to the ignorance of the writers, and which science, or right history, or personal experience has undeniably shown, are not in harmony with the facts. This is the contest which we must now meet. It is a battle for the authority of the Word of God.

It is not denied by the Christian or the critic, that many variations have found their way into the different manuscripts during the centuries; a word or a figure incorrect, sometimes a marginal note, which an annotator may have written, has crept into the text of subsequent copies. But apart from such errors, not one of which by the way effects in the slightest degree any of the essential or saving truths, the Christian church has taken the Word of God as it has come down through the ages, and has called it, as did Christ, "the truth," infallible, "the only infallible rule of faith and conduct."

There can be no doubt, that the Scriptures and Christ claim absolute trustworthiness for the Old Testament writings, which are to-day the particular object of attack. To use the words of Canon Liddon: "Our Lord set the seal of his infallible sanction upon the whole of the Old Testament. He found the Hebrew Canon as we have it to-day, and he treated it as an authority which was above discussion. Nay more, he went out of his way, if we may reverently speak thus, to sanction not a few portions which modern skepticism rejects." As an admonition against turning back, he charges his disciples to "remember Lot's wife." (Luke xvii, 32.) As a sign of his divinity in the resurrection from the dead, he appeals to the facts of Jonah's release on the third day from the whale. As a warning to the incorrigible, he holds up God's sudden overthrow of the antediluvian world by the flood.

The boast of Christianity is that it is historical. It is a religion founded on facts. If now these facts are not trustworthy, neither is the religion which depends upon them. "If Christ could be mistaken on a matter of such strictly religious importance as the value of the sacred literature of his countrymen, can he be safely trusted about anything else?" If this book tell us falsely of earthly things, how can it be depended upon when it tells us of heavenly things? When Dr. Duff overthrew the claims to divine

origin and authority of the sacred books of the Hindoos, so that now there is probably not an educated Hindoo who assigns them more than a human origin in a venerable antiquity, he found it sufficient to show that they were filled with errors concerning nature, and the things of this life, and then to retort, "Can these books tell you aright of the eternal and the spiritual, when they are so manifestly ignorant of the temporal and the natural?" If now it could be demonstrated that the Bible, has undeniably fallen into errors of wilfulness or ignorance concerning any of its statements of history, or science, or human experience, then we too should be compelled to acknowledge, as have the Hindoos, that writers who are so unreliable and ignorant in dealing with the facts of nature are not competent to teach us the more difficult and subtle things about nature's God.

The purpose of this and of several succeeding papers will be to consider this question, *Is the Bible trustworthy when tested by the clearly ascertained facts of science, or history, or human experience?* In other words—Is God's word the truth?

We will at this time confine our inquiry to the question,

IS THE BIBLE TRUSTWORTHY WHEN TESTED BY THE FACTS OF SCIENCE?

For clearly the test must be between the FACTS of nature and the FACTS of revelation, for it would be manifestly unfair to ask, that the Bible be accepted, or rejected, as the *theories* which men have invented about the facts of nature should, or should not harmonize with the *interpretations* which men have put on revelation. The authors of these theories and interpretations are men, and very fallible ; but the Author of the facts of nature and of revelation is the infallible God. And the books must harmonize, if he has written them both.

Neither must we expect to find in the Bible all the facts of nature, nor a complete system of any science, for it was given as a revelation not of the physical, but of the moral and spiritual world. Its language also ought not to be the scientific terminology of the schools, for the book is intended for all mankind, of whom the majority are unscientific and unlettered. But where the purpose, or the necessity of its writers has led them to speak of any of the facts of nature, it is fair to demand, as the price of our acceptance of Bible truth, if not scientific systems or scientific terminology, certainly strict accuracy in the fact.

If in one instance the Bible has been betrayed into the acceptance of false theories, then the whole book of that writer is discountenanced.

In two of our sciences the Bible has been led to speak with some fullness: first, of the formation and history of the earth, and, second, of the heavens. To these two, therefore, the geology and the astronomy of the Bible, our attention must be confined.

The attack of GEOLOGY upon the record of the word has been confined practically to the account of the *creation* and of the *flood.*

1. Of the creation.

Geology has succeeded in putting a much larger meaning into the word day, as used in the first chapter of Genesis, than Christians had at one time been willing to allow it, but not more than the word rightly bears. For in Hebrew, as in English, the word has the indefinite meaning of a period of time, often more or less than a strict day of twenty-four hours. A man does a day's work, is it an eight hour, or a ten hour, or a twelve hour day? Then how frequently do men exclaim, "I have never seen the like in my day!" meaning very clearly, in their lifetime. Now, the Bible uses the word "day" in just this indefinite sense, to mean some epoch, or unit of time, without clearly determining whether it is a day, or a year, or a century, or a thousand years. Job xiv, 6, speaking of the life of a man, says, "Turn from him, that he may rest, till he shall ac-accomplish, as a hireling, his day." In Gen. ii, 4, the whole period of creation is spoken of as one day. In Deut. xxxi, 17, Zech. iv, 10, John viii, 6, 2 Pet. iii, 8, the same indefinite length of "day" is indicated.

Let us now take the days of the sacred record in comparison with the epochs of Geology, and we have a most marvelous correspondence.

ACCORDING TO GEOLOGY.	ACCORDING TO THE BIBLE.
First Period: A fiery mist.	First Day: Light.
Second Period: Rains and accumulation of sediment.	Second Day: Firmament, or the separation of the waters.
Third Period: Upheaving of continents, and the appearance of marine plants.	Third Day: Appearance of dry land, and creation of plants.
Fourth Period; The dispersion of clouds, rendering sun and moon and stars visible. Plant growth.	Fourth Day: Appearance of sun and moon and stars to measure the days and seasons.
Fifth Period: Aquatic animals and birds.	Fifth Day: Aquatic animals and birds.
Sixth Period: Mammals and man.	Sixth Day: Mammals and man.

This harmony becomes all the more remarkable, when we remember the times in which the Bible was written. That it should have escaped the crude errors of the age, is conceivable only upon the recognition of the divine inspiration and revelation which Moses enjoyed. The old Egyptians, in all whose learning Moses was educated, thought that the world was hatched out of an immense egg. The Phœnicians, the East Indians, the Chinese and the Fins all preserve this tradition. According to one of the Babylonian traditions, creation is born of the marriage of Baal and Tanith. In view of these facts we can the better appreciate the decided language of Prof. Dana, the eminent geologist, when he says: "The record in the Bible is, therefore, profoundly philosophical in the scheme of creation which it presents. It is both true and divine. It is a declaration of authorship, of both creation and the Bible, on the first page of the sacred volume." "The first thought which strikes the scientific reader, (of the Mosaic account of creation), is the evident divinity, not merely in the first verse of the record, and the successive fiats, but in the while order of creation. There is so much that the most recent readings of science have for the first time explained, that the idea of man as the author becomes utterly incomprehensible. By proving the record true science pronounces it divine ; for who could have correctly narrated the secrets of eternity but God himself ?"

The second point in which Geology has attacked the Sacred Records is in the account of the FLOOD.

Huxley has boldly challenged the truthfulness of this record. He says of the flood, "it cannot have been universal, for geology knows nothing of it." "It cannot have been local for that is a physical impossibility," and such a flood as could have been local would not satisfy the Bible record. "The story is of Babylonian origin," "yet Christ evidently believed it."

Of course Christ evidently believed, that there was a flood. The traditions of every land record a flood. The Greeks, the Babylonians, the North American Indians, the Santals of India, the Hindus, the Polynesians, in fact, it is nearly impossible to find a people, whose traditions do not describe a flood, many features of which are similar to the account in Genesis. How did this tradition spread so widely, if there were not a flood over the inhabited parts of the earth destroying all men from its face? But what is tradition worth in the balances against such a positive geological statement? If the testimony of geology were clear, or a unit upon the subject, we should allow it more weight. All that can be claimed by Mr. Huxley is, that he does not know of any geological evidence of a general flood. But what Mr. Huxley has never found, others of equal ability have clearly found. Sir William Dawson, the scientist, in writing on this subject, refers with approval to the work of Howarth on "The Mammoth and the Flood," as follows: "He collects largely not only the diluvial traditions of so many races and countries, but also an immense mass of palæontological evidence, and then says, that in his judgment the whole points "to a wide-spread calamity, involving a flood on a large scale. I do not see how the historian, the archæologist, or the palæontologist can avoid making this conclusion in future a prime factor in their discussions, and I venture to think that before long it will be accepted as unanswerable."

Prof. Lyell, himself a geologist of great note, says: "In 1806 a French geologist enumerated no less than eighty theories all of which were hostile to the Scriptures," but, adds the Professor, "not one of those theories is held to-day." The best results of Geology therefore, do not impair, but rather enhance the trustworthiness of the Bible.

We turn now to ask what is the result of ASTRONOMY'S testimony concerning the Bible?

Much has been made out of the fact, that the Bible speaks of the sun's rising and setting, of his running a race through the heavens, of the blue expanse of the "firmament," as though the Bible thought that the arch above us was of solid crystal. This, it is true, is not scientific language, but the acceptance of the common forms of speech in which the multitudes refer to things as they appear. For language had taken on these forms before the revelation was made. Now, is it necessary to accuse the inspirer of the Bible of ignorance, because he chose to use such expressions? The Nautical Almanac issued by our government from the National Observatory at Washington, one of the foremost publications of the scientific world, is still in this year of our Lord, giving the times for the rising and the setting of the sun. The sky is still spoken of as a "firmament," or "the starry dome of night," or "the curtain of the heavens." Yet no one understands, that the users of these common phrases are ignorant of the fact, that there is no dome, and no curtain, and that the skies are not solid spheres in which the stars are embedded. No astronomer, wanting to be called at sunset, would say to his servant, "John, call me when the earth in her rotation upon her axis brings the meridian of our observatory to the entrance of the shadow caused by the obstruction of intervening terrestial mass between us and the light of the sun." He would say as a sensible man, "John, call me at sunset." Nothing more or less than this direct sensible statement of its facts in the language of every day use can rightly be demanded of the Bible.

The fact upon which I ask you to ponder is this, that ancient literature is filled with the crudest, and most erroneous ideas concerning astronomical subjects, but that, though the Bible writers must have been familiar with them, they are themselves never guilty of one of these errors. What power, or wisdom except God's could have given them this exemption? It is the most marvelous proof of their infallibility.

Anaximenes thought that the earth was shaped like a table, and Leucippus that it was like a drum. Pindar believed that it was supported upon adamantine columns; the Romans and Greeks believed that it rested on the shoulders of Atlas; while in India, some say, that it is supported by a snake, but others declare that the earth rests upon the back of a tortoise, and the tortoise stands upon the back of an elephant, and that the elephant's legs reach all the way down: when the elephant moves the earth quakes. Plato, Pythagoras, and Aristotle thought that the earth was a living creature; and even Augustine said, that there were no inhabitants upon the other side. Philalaus claimed, that the earth would eventually be destroyed by the waters of the moon being dashed upon it through a whirlpool in the moon's atmosphere. But the moon has, as we now know, neither water nor atmosphere.

Concerning the moon the ideas are no less laughable. Pharnaces thought that it was a mixture of fire and air. The Stoics claimed that the moon was larger than the earth, Anaximander making it nineteen times larger. Others claimed that it is a circle of fire like the sun. We now know that the moon is a dead mass much smaller than the earth, and that all its light is reflected from the sun. The Shasters, sacred books of the Hindus, declared that the moon is 50,000 times further away than the sun. The truth is that the sun is more than 90,000,000 of miles from the earth, but the moon is only about 250,000 miles distant.

Of the sun errors equally grotesque were held. Philalaus said, that it was merely a beautiful crystal reflecting the light of the earth. Epicurus taught that it was "as large as it appears, or somewhat larger or smaller." Anaxagoras however asserted that it was "as large as the whole Peloponesus," [that is about as large as the State of New Jersey]. Anaximander was daring enough, however, to maintain that the sun was twenty-eight times larger than the whole earth. But modern science has found the sun to be 1,400,000 times larger than the earth.

Diogenes said, that the stars were "pumice stones;" but Philalaus thought that they were crystals purer than diamonds. Plato made the astonishing discovery that they were "fire mixed with glue," though the famous Anaximenes had so long taught that the stars are polished nails driven in the firmament of heaven to fasten it on. Of these stars the ancients thought that there were 1,000; the Bible alone saying that they are without number. The most recent researches of science find them practically innumerable. Every time a more powerful glass is turned toward the skies, new stars are revealed. Comets were the souls of good men on their way to heaven. The Milky Way was to them an old and unused pathway of the sun, or, as others thought, the road upon which the gods passed back and forth from heaven to earth. While the utmost reach of stellar space is such that an anvil, so Hesiod says, could fall from the stars to the earth in nine days, and from the earth to the abyss in nine days more.

Yet not one of all these common errors finds a place in the Bible. Where it speaks it speaks truth. In its earliest book, Job, are astronomical statements which though contrary to the accepted thought of the day, are in most striking harmony with recent knowledge. Instead of resting the earth on the backs of men, or of elephants, or of snakes, as all the heathen seemed to do, Job says, xxvi: 7, "He stretcheth out the north over the empty place, and hangeth the earth upon nothing," just where modern astronomy has discovered that it is hung. But one of the most remarkable discoveries of astronomy is foreshadowed in Job xxxviii 31, "Canst thou bind the sweet influences of Pleiades, or loose the bands of Orion?" It is now discovered that the whole solar system is slowly passing away from the constellation of Orion, and is being drawn toward the Pleiades; around which all the systems of the heavens seem to move, in a mighty orbit, as though sweeping in the cycles of eternity around the throne of God.

It would not do to close without acknowledging my indebtedness, all through the latter part of this paper, to that admirable work of Dr. Townsend, of the University of Boston, "The Bible and Other Ancient Literature in the Nineteenth Century," and by refering all who may care to trace the effect of our knowledge of Zoology, Physiology, Botany upon the trustworthiness of the Bible, to its pages.

In uttering the conculsions of my own studies on this subject, I cannot find fitter words than those of the renowned, Sir John Herschel, England's great astronomer. "All human discoveries seem to be ma le only for the purpose of confirming more and more strongly the truths contained in the Holy Scriptures."

Is the Bible Trustworthy When Tested by the Best Results of Historical Research?

BY THE REV. WILLIAM P. SWARTZ.

✢ PART II. ✢

"THY WORD IS TRUE FROM THE BEGINNING." Ps. cxix:160.

It would be very interesting to take up and consider in successive discourses the confirmations of the Bible, which arise from the researches in Egypt, and Babylonia, and Assyria, and Charchemish; indeed, to each we might profitably devote a morning, but the press of other subjects will not allow us to go so thoroughly. "The research of the spade," as Schliemann called it, gives a testimony to the minute accuracy of the Word of the Book, that must silence every unbeliever who studies these results carefully. Within the present century the development of historical criticism has succeeded in separating between the myth and the true in ancient Roman and Greek history. Until in comparatively recent years the myth of Romulus and Remus was accepted as history of equal credit with the accounts of the Punic wars; and the legends of Perseus, and the wanderings of the Odyssey were accepted as no less true than the records of Herodotus. But under the more careful scrutiny to which modern historians have put their facts, much of the old history has rightly been relegated to the realm of myth, just as the errors of former ages have been superseded by the advances of science.

It was neither possible nor desirable, that the Bible should be exempt from this searching criticism. If it is God's word, as we claim, no advance of true knowledge can in any way discredit it. If at any point the Bible is vulnerable to the criticism of human scholarship, it would most naturally be in the field of history, for the Bible is very largely a history of God's dealings with the world in the preparation of redemption. Whatever pleas may have been raised to defend the Bible for a lack of scientific language,—because it is not a text book of science, cannot be advanced here with propriety, because the Bible is a history. Rather, it is God's revelation of himself in human history. As Dr. Ecob says, "every event is a syllable breaking from the lips of God. Every epoch in affairs is a completed sentence of his thought, and the great stream of human history is God's endless revelation of himself." The purpose of the Bible is to take the events of history, and to show man their meaning. But if the facts given in the Bible are not historically true, they have no meaning; the revelation of God in false history is a false revelation. The same necessity that demanded the giving of the revelation of this book, requires its preservation. But it could not be preserved, except as its facts were transmitted from age to age without essential error. If the Bible is to be an infallible rule of faith and practice, it must also be true history. And it is !

The history of the Bible has been fiercely assailed, but it has not in any point, of which I am aware, been shown untrustworthy. The mythical theory of Strauss, aided as it was by the efforts of Bauer and his school to assign late dates for the composition of the Gospels from 130 A. D. to 200 A. D., is now ancient history; though not much over half a century old, it is no longer possessed of any credit or influence among scholars. In more recent days the trustworthiness of the Penteteuch has been attacked; and as Bauer sought to serve the infidelity of Strauss and Renan by his critical theory of the gospels, so certain among us seek to undermine the historical accuracy and trustworthiness of the Old Testament books by assigning to them later dates than those which have heretofore been unquestioningly accepted. It is just at this opportune time that God is revealing out of the earth, in exhumed records of the remote past, such a substantiation of His word, as is fast driving the historical critic to acknowledge with wonder the strict accuracy of the Bible. Dr. Wilson, in speaking of the results of archæological studies in Egypt, says, what might truthfully be said of the recent researches in every field, "The whole monumental wonders and antiquities of the land seem to have been preserved, as if for the express purpose of evincing the authenticity and illustrating the narratives of the Bible; every single allusion of which, either to the circumstances of the people or the country, is seen to have the minutest consistency with the truth,—so strikingly so, indeed, as to have attracted the attention of every Egyptian antiquary."

The testimony of Sir William Dawson, the Canadian scientist, is to the same effect. In a late address he said: "There can be no doubt that within recent years a large amount of work on the part of surveyors, excavators and archæologists has been throwing light on the older Hebrew books and remarkably vindicating their historical truth. The Ordnance Survey of Sinai has confirmed signally the topographical accuracy of the books of Exodus and Numbers, though its force is scarcely yet appreciated by linguistic scholars. The late Professor Palmer has extended the evidence to the North, and I have myself ascertained the geological and topographical truth of the narrative relating to Egypt. My own studies of the region of the Dead Sea have enabled me to vindicate the accuracy of the narrative of the destruction of the cities of the plain, and recent discoveries in Chaldea have unearthed corroborative evidence of the battle of Abraham with the Euphratean kings. The excavations at Tanis, Taphanes, Rameses and Pithom, the Tel el Amama tablets, and multitudes of other Egyptian facts, have all tended in the same direction. The excavation at Lachish, the ruins of the ancient Minean cities of South Arabia, the monument of the Hittites and the extension of the evidence of literary work and education to times long antecedent to Moses in Egypt, in Arabia, in Syria and in Chaldea all tend in the same direction.''

But these quotations must suffice to establish the fact, that the most recent and the most exact results of history are only confirmatory of the truth of the sacred record.

It will be our duty, in as far as the time permits, to notice those points in which the accuracy of the Bible had been denied, and upon which there has been found some record from the monuments. In every instance, of which I am aware, these records have substantiated the one book, which shall never lack enemies or friends.

Of the discrepancies which it is alleged exist between the different parts of the Bible, it is not necessary for me now to speak. They are all explainable; and the difficulty has generally arisen from the ignorance of the reader. Take one as a sample of all the rest. In John xix:14, "and it was the preparation of the passover and about the sixth hour, and he [Pilate] said unto the Jews, behold your King." But in Mark xv:25, "And it was the third hour and they crucified him." If he was still in the judgment hall at the sixth hour, how could he have been crucified in the third? Even Strauss admits, that Mark used the Jewish reckoning, and that John used the Roman.

THE BABYLONIAN TESTIMONY.

One of the Bible stories very often discredited is that of the tower of Babel, and the confusion of tongues. But there have been found in the excavations at Babylon cuneiform inscriptions evidently

referring to this very incident. "We can read in the wedge-shaped letters of a 'mound' destroyed in a night, while Anu 'confounded great and small on the mound' and made 'strange their counsels.' '' (Bible Verified p. 236.)

In 2 Kings xx:2, and in Isaiah xxxix:1, it is said, that Merodach Baladan, King of Babylon, sent letters and a present to Hezekiah when he was sick. But Babylon was in the time of Hezekiah an Assyrian province, and there was no other mention in history of any such king in Babylon. It was therefore, with great confidence, that the critics of the Bible said, there was no such character as this Merodach Baladan. But more recently there has been found in the Chronicle of Eusebius a fragment of Berosus, whose history of Babylon was written over 2,000 years ago, in which we are informed, that Merodach Baladan was an usurper, who reigned independently for about six months, and was then over-thrown by Sennacherib. Thus again are the critics wrong, and the "word is true from the beginning.''

There is found also a striking confirmation of God's judgment upon Nebuchadnezzar. "They shall drive thee from among men, and thy dwelling shall be with the beasts of the field: they shall make thee to eat grass as oxen, and seven times shall pass over thee until thou know that the most High ruleth in the kingdom of men, and giveth it to whomsoever he will." Dan. iv, 42.

An inscription now in the East India House at London, according to Col. Rawlinson, describes the works of Nebuchadnezzar at Babylon and Bersippa. In the midst of the list occurs a remarkable passage, which the decipherer could not but regard as the official version of the incident of which Daniel gives us the fuller and more intelligent account. For breaking off abruptly in the account of the architectural wonders of Babylon, it denounces the astrologers, saying, "The king's heart was hardened against them. He would grant no benefactions for religious purposes. He intermitted the worship of Merodach, and put an end to the sacrifices of victims. He labored under the effects of enchantment." Then follows much more which is indistinct, but a little further on the narrative of the architectural wonders of Babylon is resumed. So must we exclaim with the Psalmist, "Thy word is true from the beginning."

Again: profane historians relate that the capture of Babylon took place under Nabonnedus, not under Belshazzar as Daniel says. Skeptics used to enlarge upon this, as they did upon other statements, which they regarded as erroneous. For the oldest secular historian of Babylon says, that the last king of Babylon was not in the city when it was taken by the Persians; but that he was afterward taken prisoner at Bersippa, and was treated with the greatest consideration by Cyrus. Here then was direct and irreconcilable contradiction.

But a few years ago there was found near Babylon, what is known as the Nabonnedus Cylinder on which are these words: "As for me, Nabonnedus, the King of Babylon, preserve me from sinning against thy great divinity, and grant me the gift of a life of long days; and plant in the heart of Beishazzar, the eldest son, the offspring of my heart, reverence for thy great divinity, and never may he incline to sin; with fullness of life may he be

satisfied." So we see that this last king known to profane history had a son Belshazzar; and Sir Henry Rawlinson has found at Ur of the Chaldees, near Babylon, records, which establish beyond a doubt the fact that Nabonnedus had associated Belshazzar with himself upon the throne. Of Nabonnedus it was true as the ancient Berosus had said; but it was also true as Daniel relates of the capture of Babylon, and the death of Belshazzar. Here too is the explanation of a fact which had long puzzled students. In the narrative in Daniel, Belshazzar makes Daniel the third in the government, not the second, as one would have supposed, but the third ; and that because there were already two on the throne. So while there is no mention of Nabonnedus in the sacred narrative, a single numeral, which might have been changed by some puzzled transcriber of the book in all these thousands of years, has been preserved to display, as it does now, the absolute accuracy of the Bible. Yes, God's "word is true from the beginning."

Uninspired historians have spoken of Cyrus as a Persian monotheist, and, therefore, much more disposed to acknowledge the one God of the Jews, and to honor him in returning the captivity of Judah. It required some strange explanation on the part of commentators of Isaiah xxi, 2; "Go up, O Elam; besiege, O Media." It was generally said, that Cyrus was a Persian, and that Elam was in the height of the Persian empire one of the provinces, and that by the figure Synechdoche, the part was put for the whole. But now we know from the clay tablets dug out of the earth, that Cyrus was an Elamite, and a polytheist. So that the word of

God is true without any explanation. Yes it is "true from the beginning."

THE ASSYRIAN TESTIMONY.

In the excavations at Ninevah a whole library has been dug from the earth. The royal collection of Assurbanipal, the Sardanaplus of the Greeks, after being buried for 2,500 years has been brought to the light. It consists principally of bricks, upon which the records were written when they were soft clay. They were then burned to almost the hardness of stone. There is already much more of this Assyrian literature than of the whole of the Old Testament. It would be interesting to recount the labors, by which this, a new language in our day, was deciphered, and its treasures put at the service of God. But we must forbear. The corroborations of the Bible to be derived from these writings of the remote past, are no less remarkable than in the case of the Babylonian remains. I can mention this morning but two of them.

Isaiah says that "Sargon, King of Syria," captured "Ashdod." For 2,500 years this was the only record of such a king. More than once has profane history, therefore, said, that the Bible was mistaken here. But now there has been found a cylinder bearing the name of this very king, and describing the expedition of which Isaiah speaks. Sargon's existence also clears up difficulties in the tenth and eleventh chapters of Isaiah, which did not apply to any known conqueror.

On these cylinders we read also of Sennecherib and Hezekiah. There is one other contribution against the critics, and to the relief of the Christian, which these records afford and which I cannot forbear mentioning this morning. We are told in the Bible, that Ezar-haddon, king of Assyria, "took Mannassah in chains and bound him in fetters;" and there is added in Chronicles, and "carried him to Babylon." But Ninevah was the Assyrian capital, not Babylon, which had been overthrown and despoiled. It was as if some one should read in the far future, that Queen Victoria took the Prince of India captive, and carried him to Berlin. Just such seemed the Bible's mistake. But these monuments tell us that Ezar-haddon repaired Babylon and made it one of his chief seats of government. So, "Thy word, O God, is true from the beginning."

THE TESTIMONY CONCERNING THE HITTITES.

Among the Canaanites, whose possessions were taken by the Israelites, when they occupied Canaan, are named the Hittites. It was these people who had sold a grave to Abraham. The Bible represented them a great people. In 2 Kings the Syrians are represented as saying, "Lo, the king of Israel hath hired against us the kings of the Hittites, and the kings of the Egyptians." But Prof. F. W. Newman, brother of the Cardinal, in his history of the Hebrew Monarchy published in 1857, claimed that this was "unhistorical," because the Hittites were too insignificant a tribe to be mentioned along with the powerful Egyptians. But now their capital, Carchemish, has opened its bosom, and is showing that these Hittites were one of the powerful people of antiquity. They contested the supremacy of the East, not only with Assyria, but also with Egypt. They maintained a long struggle with the latter country, when it was in its prime under Rameses the Great; and were after it able to treat with Egypt on equal terms. The treaty of peace entered into between the "great king of Keeta," i. e. of the Hittites, and the "great prince of Egypt," is preserved to this day on the walls of the temple at Karnak in Egypt.

No sooner is this difficulty settled, than another arises. Dr. Cheyne in his articles in the last edition of the Encyclopedia Britannica vol. xii: p. 25 says of the Hittites, "They were a warlike and powerful nation, whose centre lay in the far north of Syria, * * The Hittites are repeatedly mentioned among the tribes which inhabited Canaan before the Israelites, but the lists of these pre-Israelitish populations cannot be taben as strictly historical documents. * * If then," he continues, "we employ the familiar name, Hittite, * * let it be understood that by this term we do not indicate one of the Canaanitish people conquered by the Israelites, but an extra Palestinian race capable of holding its own even against Egypt and Assyria." At the first the Bible could not be true for it represented these Hittites as great enough to be associated with the Egyptians. Now so reputable and scholarly a work as the Encyclopedia Britannica errs in supposing the Hittites so great, that the Israelitish hordes could not have conquered any of their possessions in Palestine, where it is acknowledged that they probably had communities. Once again the monuments come to the support of the word of God, and show that the Hittites waged war for eighty years with Seti I. and Rameses, with whom Moses was contemporary, until peace was concluded because both nations were so exhausted

that they could not fight longer. In this state they were not able to defend themselves against the Israelites, who took their Palestinian possessions. That the armies of the conquest did not conquer, and overthrow the Hittite empire itself, is clearly implied in the scriptures from the fact that it is mentioned hundreds of years after the conquest as one of the great powers of Asia, of whose kings even Syria, the scourge, was afraid. I shall look for a later edition of the Encyclopedia Britannica to modify the statements of this article, "For God's word is true from the beginning."

But why continue? These instances could be multiplied many fold. We could show how one seeming difficulty after another has been cleared up, as the reliable testimony, which God has saved to overwhelm the skepticism, and to silence the caviling of these later days, is gathered from the ruins of ages. The very stones are crying out to the support of the Master's word. As we have seen by the few instances examined this morning, time after time have adverse criticism and a too confident unbelief been compelled to acknowledge the truth of the Bible and their own mistake. I do not know of a single instance were a statement of Bible history has been undeniably disproved.

Negative criticism, the mythical theory, and the learning of the Tuebingen school, skepticism and unbelief have hurled themselves repeatedly against this book, which Gladstone has called the "Impregnable Rock of Sacred Scripture." They have not broken it, but have been broken by it. To use the words of Prof. Sayce, the eminent Oxford orientalist, "The same spirit of skepticism, which had rejected the early legends of Greece and Rome, had laid its hands also on the Old Testament, and had determined that the sacred histories themselves were but a collection of myths and fables. But suddenly as with the wand of a magician, the ancient Eastern world has been awakened to life by the spade of the explorer and the patient skill of the decipherer, and we now find ourselves in the presence of monuments which bear the names or recount the deeds of the heroes of Scripture." (Quoted in the Bible Verified p. 247) "Though three thousand years have passed away," says another writer, "the very scenes of the Old Testament are here faithfully reproduced, while, as if to confound the folly of modern skepticism, the famous capitals, which were the seats of mighty kings, 'when Egypt with Assyria, strove in wealth and luxury,' have been summoned from their grave." (Rev. Henry Tullidge, in Triumphs of the Bible, p. 409.) The stones have cried out, and what do they say? "Thy word is truth," O God, "Thy word is true from the beginning."

Is the Bible Trustworthy as tested by the failure or the fulfillment of its prophecy?

BY THE REV. WILLIAM P. SWARTZ.

✦ **PART III.** ✦

We have also a more sure word of prophecy; whereunto ye do well to take heed.

For the prophecy came not in old time by the will of man: but holy men of God spake as they were moved by the Holy Ghost.

2 Peter 1:19, 21.

In Deut. the Bible lays down for itself and for all prophecy this test, that, if the thing which has been prophesied does not come to pass in its time, then that prophecy is not of the Lord. Let us read the words: "When a prophet speaketh in the name of the Lord, if the thing follow not, nor come to pass, that is the thing which the Lord hath not spoken, but the prophet hath spoken it presumptuously." Deut. 18: 22. If now we apply this principle to the sacred writings of Christendom, we must say of the Bible, if its prophecies do not come to pass in their time, then this book is not the Word of God ; but if, on the other hand, its prophecies are fulfilled in the most marvellous and complete manner, then does this fulfillment become God's seal of authority set on the whole book.

The prophecies of the Bible are so numerous and so daring in their details, that if the author of these books be not God, infinite in wisdom, to whom the things which are to be are even as the things which have been, certain and known, but if men were their authors, then the failures of their predictions must long ago have brought confusion upon all who trusted in them.

"For God frustrateth the tokens of liars and maketh diviners mad; he turneth wise men backward and maketh their knowledge foolish ; but he confirmeth the word of His servants, and performeth the counsels of his messengers." Isaiah, 44:25, 26. If any where the armour of this word can be pierced, and its trustworthiness disproved, it would be in the failure of its prophecy. For, to use the words of Bishop Foster, its prophecy "opens in the first chapter of the Bible, and like a stream deepening and widening as it flows, swells into a vast river as it descends the centuries, until at the end of four thousand years it utters its closing and most sublime sentence in the last chapter of the Apocalypse. In its course it sweeps through all time, now adumbrating the fate of nations and world-renowned cities and empires, anon sketching the destiny of men and systems, and having for its chief and greatest function to trace the rise and spread of the divine kingdom on earth,—the coming of the Son of God, the wonders of his mission, his matchless character and matchless deeds,the struggles and dversities of its course in its beginnings, until, gathering resistless strength, it finally sweeps away all opposing systems of superstition and wrong, ascends the throne of the world and inaugurates an era of universal peace and happiness among men; then, rising with a bolder flight, it depicts the closing scene of earth's history, the final coming of the Son of Man, the transformation of the physical word itself, and the magnificent dawn of the everlasting age. One only needs to be caught up in the roll of its mighty events to feel that he stands amid the unutterable sublimities of an infinite plan, that he is following the march of events to a consummation worthy of· the majesty of God. We occupy a stand point in the middle of the amazing scheme. Behind us in the six thousand years of the world's history is a cycle of completed events, filling the exact measure of the chart up to date ; around us are the proofs of its complete fulfillment up till now, the unfulfilled comes to meet us." (The Supernatural Book, page 74.)

All prophecy is not yet fulfilled; some of it, we are told by learned scholars of our day, never can be fulfilled. Is the Bible therefore untrustworthy ? We ought to remember that in the great sum of absolute prophecy, there is much contingent prediction such as the prophecy against Nineveh which God pronounced through his reluctant messenger, Jonah, "After

forty days" Nineveh was not destroyed. The contingency which alone could divert the calamity arose and Nineveh was given respite. God has himself declared this principle in Jer. xviii:7. "At what instant I shall speak concerning a nation and concerning a kingdom, to pluck up and to pull down, and to destroy it ; if that nation against whom I have pronounced, turn from their evil, I will repent of the evil that I thought to do unto them."

The prophecy whose fulfillment has been thus averted has nevertheless served its purpose as surely as any of that absolute prophecy whose marvelous fulfillment history has recorded. For the minatory prophecy is given not that it may be fulfilled, but that it may not be fulfilled. For God having, as it is said in Ezekiel xxxiii:11, no pleasure in the death of a sinner, but in his turning from his ways, the first and chief purpose of the prophetic announcement of the divine judgment is to lead to repentance, and hence if the repentance takes place, the prophecy has served its purpose and the judgment is averted. Neither was it the exclusive privilege of Israel to repent, but any nation which heard God's word could avert its calamity by forsaking its evil way and seeking pardon. In this connection the words of Jerome deserve careful consideration, "Nor does it inevitably follow, that since the prophet predicts, it will come to pass, because he has predicted. For he has not prophesied, in order that it may come to pass, but lest it come to pass. Neither since God speaks is it necessary that it should follow because he has threatened, but he threatens in order that he who is threatened may be brought to repentance, and that the evil may not befall which would have come had the words of God been despised.'' [From Jerome's comments on Ez. xxxiii: 11.]

The first purpose of prophecy, therefore, is not to attest the divine origin of the teachings of any of the prophets, or of the volume of the book ; this use of prophecy, though legitimate, is incidental. The great underlying purpose of prophecy is the good of the people —to restrain them from a wicked course and its consequent destruction. Prophecy is, therefore, the mercy of God going before his justice for the salvation, not for the destruction of men. And God is better pleased when the fulfillment of the prophecy need not follow. When we look at the words of the prophets in this light, which I assure you is the right light, we see that the prophecies are not merely records of events to come, but they reveal the great underlying principles of the Divine government, and are of present vital significance, rightly demanding our closest study and most prayerful observance.

In bringing, therefore, the testimony of Prophecy to the trustworthiness of the Scriptures it becomes necessary to enquire whether the prophecy is one which should have been fulfilled. Then, whether those prophecies which have been fulfilled afford any indubitable evidence, that they have proceeded from a real fore-knowledge of what was to come to pass, or whether they are merely shrewd and lucky guesses, which men of acknowledged judgment and keen insight could take without a divine revelation. The Scriptures themselves are full of declarations, that the spoken or written word is the word of God. (See text.) Therefore,

the whole fabric must stand or fall, as the matching of the event to the prophecy shall either prove or disprove this claim.

Let us now take some of the prophecies upon special subjects, and notice the number of persons who have contributed a share to their completion ; the years which have separated the different prophets not only from one another, but also from the events of which they prophesied ; the fullness of details which they have given, and the improbability of any such event when the prophecies were spoken; and then examining the record of history let us ask ourselves, whether the event and prophecy join to attest the trustworthiness of the whole record. ''For when a prophet shall speak in the name of the Lord, if the thing follow not, nor come to pass, that is the thing which the Lord hath not spoken.'' Has he, or has he not spoken this word ? If he has spoken it, then it is all true, and trustworthy, and like God it is always right.

The chief subject of Old Testament prophecy is Christ. Every feature of Christ's life on the earth was foretold with astonishing accuracy. ''The details scattered through so many prophets, yet all converging in him, the race, nation, tribe, family, birth-place, miracles, humiliation, death, crucifixion with the wicked yet association with the rich at death, resurrection, extension of his seed the church, are so numerous that their minute conformity with the subsequent fact can only be explained by believing that the prophets were moved by the Holy Ghost to foretell the event. What is overwhelmingly convincing is, the Jews are our sacred librarians who attest the prophets as written ages before, and

4

who certainly would not have corrupted them to confirm Jesus' Messianic claims which they reject.

"The details moreover are so complicated and seemingly inconsistent that before the event it would seem impossible to make them coincide in one person, 'a Son,' yet 'the everlasting Father;' 'a child,' yet 'the mighty God;' 'the Prince of Peace,' 'sitting on the throne of David,' yet 'coming when the sceptre shall depart from Judah;' 'David's Son,' yet 'David's Lord;' a 'Prophet' and a 'priest,' and yet also a 'King;' the one who 'upholds all things by the word of his power,' yet the 'servant of God;' 'the judge of all,' yet he upon whom 'the Lord hath laid the iniquity of us all;' the 'Messiah cut off,' yet given by the Ancient of Days, 'an everlasting dominion;' one 'who is despised and rejected of men,' and yet coming into possession of a 'kingdom that all people, nations, and languages should serve him.' The only key which opens this immensely complicated lock is the life and work of Jesus, so faithfully portrayed in the Gospels, a life which began on the earth some four hundred years after the last of the prophets had gone to heaven.'' (Fausett's Bible Cyclopedia, 1892.)

If there were not another prophecy in the Scriptures, these would alone establish their divine origin with the incontestable certainty of a demonstration. Their challenge has been before the world for 1800 years. Ancient skeptics could not meet it. Before it modern infidelity is dumb. It cannot be met. "It is God's own witness to the divinity of his own word." (Foster.)

But if it be objected by any one, that the confirmation of the prophets is found in a book especially written to show that these pro-

phecies were fulfilled in one, Jesus of Nazareth, this cannot invalidate any point of the argument, unless it be also shown that the writers of these Gospels have entered into collusion to leave us a false record, unhistorical and untrustworthy. This has never been shown, and never can. Yet we are not dependent upon the New Testament records for evidence of the most complete fulfillment of the details, —the very minutia of many and diverse prophecies.

Take now the prophecy concerning the Jews, as it is found in Deut. xxviii. This was spoken 1450 B. C. by Moses as a farewell address to Israel. He had led them out of Egypt; he had suffered for them and with them in the wilderness forty years; he had now come to the borders of Caanan, and had been told by God, that he should not himself pass over the river, but must go up into the mountain and die. Before departing on that last journey, he gathers all the people before him, that they may receive his dying charge. "All history furnishes nothing parallel in pathos and sublimity.'' Thus after recounting God's wonderful dealings with them, and giving them again the law which was commanded for their observance, he warns them "but it shall come to pass, if thou wilt not hearken unto the voice of the Lord thy God, * * * that all these cursings shall come upon thee." See Deut. xxvii:45-53; 62-67.

Jeremiah, Hosea and Ezekiel unite to declare such calamities as no other people ever survived, and yet they say, "I will make a full end of the nations whither I have driven thee; but I will not make a full end of thee." This is the prophecy. What does history say? Josephus, himself a Jew, gives a narrative of the siege of Titus in which Jerusalem was destroyed and the fulfilment of these prophecies begun. How well are these Romans indicated in the verses read! A "people of fierce countenance," "eagles flying," "yoke is iron." They laid siege to Jerusalem. They destroyed its walls, and slew its inhabitants. Verse 28, speaks of "hunger," "thirst," "nakedness," "want of all things;" and verse 53 says, "thou shalt eat the fruit of thine own body, the flesh of thy sons and of thy daughters * * in the siege and in the straitness where with thine enemies shall straiten thee." This hunger, and thirst and want of all things, Josephus describes, even to the eating of their own children. These are his words: "The famine began to extend its progress, and to devour the people by whole houses and families. The upper rooms were full of women and children that were dying by famine; and the lanes of the city were full of the dead bodies of the aged. * * *

The children also and the young men wandered about the market-places like shadows, all swelled with the famine, and fell down dead wherever their misery seized them. * * A deep silence also and a kind of deadly gloom, had seized upon the city. While yet the robberies were still more terrible than these miseries. For they break open those houses which were none other than the graves of dead bodies, and plundered them of what they had; and carrying off the coverings of their bodies, went out laughing, and tried the points of their swords in their dead bodies; and in order to prove what mettle they were made of, they thrust some of those through that still lay alive

upon the ground. * * Now of those that perished by famine in the city, the number was prodigious; and the miseries they underwent were unspeakable." Then he relates what he calls, the most horrible matter, which "has no parallel in all history." How a woman of "eminent family and of wealth" (compare Deut. 28:56) in her desperation killed, and roasted, and ate the flesh of her own son, "whereupon," he adds, "the whole city was full of this horrid action."

When at last Jerusalem was taken by Titus, and he examined the walls of the inner city, according to Josephus who was with him at the time, Titus "expressed himself after the following manner: "We certainly have had God for our assistant in this war and it was no other than God who ejected the Jews out of these fortifications. For what could the hands of men, or any machines do towards overthrowing these towers?" Then as though he intended to fulfill the prediction of Christ, that "not one stone shall be left upon another" of these mighty walls, it is recorded, "that he demolished the city entirely, and overthrew its walls."

Of the inhabitants of the city, Josephus tells us that 1,100,000 perished in the siege. Those sallying out of the city were taken and crucified before the walls, often as many as four hundred in a single day, in so much as that there became a scarcity of wood for crosses. How terribly was the curse of those who cried, Away with him! Crucify him! Crucify him! His blood be upon us and upon our children! —how terribly was this imprecation visited upon them! Many others were slain after the fall of of the city. Only 97,000 remained to be carried into captivity; some were sent as presents to the provinces where they were slain in the arena, and the vast majority were sent by ships to work in the mines of Egypt, according to the prophecy. (Compare Deut. 28:68)

Thus began the fulfillment of the prophecy 1800 years ago, and it is still being fulfilled under our very eyes. "They were rooted out of their land," as Isaiah had predicted, "in anger, and in wrath, and in great indignation." "And the Lord has scattered them among all people, from one of the earth even unto the other." Such a like calamity no other people ever survived. Yet it is part of the promise that they shall be preserved for further sorrows and distresses in the lands whether they were exiled. [Deut. xxviii:64-65.] and afterward they shall turn to Christ, and come again, a great number, to the land of their fathers, too many for the land, for it shall be too narrow to contain them. It would require a resume of the history of all nations to show with what wonderful accuracy this prophecy has been fulfilled. It must suffice to say, that the prophecy and the history are one in character, in scope, and in issue. The Jews have been scattered throughout the whole earth ; yet they have remained everywhere a distinct race—a people without a country; they have been despoiled everywhere, yet never destroyed; "the most wonderful and amazing facts, such as never occurred among any other people, form the ordinary narrative of their history," and fulfill literally the prophecies concerning them. Whoever seeks a miracle may here behold a "sign and a wonder" than which there cannot be a greater. And the Christian may from the test of fulfilled prophecy, challenge every candid man

to acknowledge, that the minutest statements of this word are true, because it is God's word. "Heaven and earth shall pass away but one jot or one tittle shall in no wise pass from the law, till all be fulfilled." Matt. 5:18.

The foreknowledge of God knows no bounds. His prophecy was not limited to the future of the Jews or the kingdom of Christ. Therefore, to deepen the impression, which doubtless has already been made, notice how minutely the prophecies which were spoken against some other great nations of antiquity have been fulfilled.

We will examine first the prophecies against Babylon, or rather because they are so many, only a few of them. See Is. xiii:19-22. (Compare Jeremiah 50.)

When these prophecies were spoken, Babylon was the mistress of the world, the hammer of the nations. When Jeremiah spoke, she was just leading the people of God away into the Babylonian captivity. Two hundred and fifty years after Isaiah, Herodotus wrote of Babylon upon his visit: "Its extent, its beauty, its magnificence, surpass all that has come within my knowledge." It included at the time of the visit of Herodotus 225 sq. miles within its walls, while London to-day covers only 122 sq. miles and New York only 41 sq. miles. Its walls, its hanging garden, its great artificial lake thirty-five feet deep and 160 miles in circumference, its broad avenues and its stately palaces and its great wealth, for it was called "the golden," made it at the time of the prophet "the glory of the Kingdoms, the city upon the rivers," seemingly superior to the decay of time, or the attack of enemies. Yet as early as 20 B. C. Strabo tells us, that "the site of

Babylon is a vast desolation." And so it has remained all through the centuries. Jerusalem w h i c h it destroyed has been rebuilt and is inhabited, but not so Babylon, for it shall "never be inhabited," says Isaiah. Layard writes, "The site of Babylon is a naked and hideous waste. Owls start from the scanty thickets, and foul jackals stalk through the furrows." For two months in the year by reason of the overflow of the Euphrates the site of Babylon is an inland sea, and the other ten months it is a dry and scorching plain. Neither Arab nor shepherd will pitch a tent upon its site even for a single night. "I cannot portray," says Captain Mignau in his travels, "the overpowering sensation of reverential awe that possessed my mind while contemplating the extent and magnitude of ruin and desolation on every side." "It is impossible to behold the scene and not to be reminded how exactly the predictions of Isaiah and Jeremiah have been fulfilled, even in the appearance Babylon is doomed to present: that she should never be inhabited; that the Arabian should not pitch his tent there; that she should become heaps; that her cities should be a desolation, a dry land and a wilderness."

Old Moab, whose captivity God has promised to "bring again in the latter days," probably for the sake of that sweet Moabitess, whose faith and love made her the grandmother of King David, and the ancestress of Christ,—upon Moab is now accomplished the cry of the prophet, "Give wings unto Moab, that it may flee and get away; for the cities thereof shall be desolate, without any to dwell therein. Moab is spoiled and gone out of her cities." Says Mr. Graham, the

traveller, in speaking of B e t h-Gamul, the very city named in conection with this prophecy, "It is still very perfect. We walked about through the streets and entered every house, and opened the stone doors, and saw the rooms as if they had just been left; and then thought that we were in the dwelling place of a people which for 2,500 years had ceased to be a people; yet these cities of Moab .are still so perfect that they might be inhabited to-morrow." The remnant of the Moabites is still to be found, as the prophet predicted, "like doves making their nests in the sides of the mouths of the caves." They are ready to come again into these cities, when God brings them, for he has promised, "I will bring again the captivity of Moab in the latter days."

But I must close, though we have journeyed only on the edges of this vast and interesting subject. Allow me to refer you for further r e a d i n g to Keith's "T h e Demonstration of Christianity," and to Bishop Foster's "The Supernatural Book," where you may find traced the fulfillment of many more prophecies, no less remarkable than these which we have considered this morning,—prophecies spoken against the city of Samaria, now a garden in "the midst of a field;" and again Gaza, of which the fires, prophesied years before, have left here and there blackened marbles as the only evidences of her once magnificent palaces; and against Lebanon, "ashamed and hewn down;" for only four or five of her stately cedars remain, says Volney, "to challenge our admiration of its past;" and against Egypt, once the first kingdom of the earth, but as God spake by the mouth of Ezekiel, "she has been wasted by the hand of the strangers," for the Persians, the Macedonians, the Greeks, the Romans, the Arabs, and the unspeakable Turk, have spoiled her, until she is now as predicted, "the basest of the kingdoms." Of Tyre, and of Nineveh, of Edom and of Philistia, as the prophets have prophesied, so is it accomplished. God hath spoken, and he hath performed it. No evidence to the absolute trustworthiness of the Bible is stronger, none so incontrovertable as this. Mighty empires have risen, and flourished, and decayed; dynasties has been established and overthrown; nations have passed away and others have been born; languages have perished with the peoples which spoke them; old systems of science and philosophy have proved untrue, and have been superseded; new worlds have been discovered, and new arts have been developed: but amid all the changes of the ages, God's word standeth unchanged and unchanging: Though it has portrayed with prophetic, yet unerring accuracy the rise and fall of nations, and of religions, and of systems, it has itself remained unaffected and unshaken. But why has it thus stood? There is but one answer: because it is God's infallible word.

"For the prophecy came not in old time by the will of man: but holy men of old spake as they were moved by the Holy Ghost." "Wherefore we have a more sure word of prophecy; whereunto ye do well to take heed, as unto a light shining in a dark place, until the day dawn, and the day star arise in your hearts."

Is the Bible Trustworthy When Tested by Human Experience?

BY THE REV. WILLIAM P. SWARTZ.

✛ PART IV. ✛

"If any man will do his will, he shall know of the doctrine, whether it be of God." John vii:17.

We have already put the Bible to the test of absolute accuracy in its science, its history and its prophecy; and we have seen, that in every department it has evinced a more than human trustworthiness We would now apply to it the test of human experience. Has man found that its statements are true, or false, as he has tested it by this experience of his own nature and its needs, of his present condition and his future possibilities?

Whatever it may contain of science, or of history, or of prophecy, the great reason of the Bible's existence, if we may take its own account of itself, is to reveal man unto himself, to show him his relation to God, and the wonderful possibilities of his nature in God. If there has been any revelation of or appeal to the facts of nature, it has been made for this purpose. If there is a history running through this book, it is that man may better know himself, and the character and demands of the Almighty. If it has employed prophecy, it is for the purpose of turning man away from that which it says is evil, or of comforting and encouraging him in the path of righteousness. The Bible is emphatically for man.

Now it is right to expect in such a book, if its claims to divine authorship are true, that it will meet all the necessities of man's nature; it must be so complete as to leave no essential truth unrevealed; it must never be superseded by any inventions or discoveries of men; it must always be in advance of his highest attainments in civilization and righteousness; it must commend itself to him by such evidences of truth as would convince a candid mind in any other department of knowledge; its province would be to emphasize the spiritual, and thus indirectly to promote the comfort and prosperity of man intellectually and physically; from its teachings and spirit should develop the noblest traits of character, a stronger faith in the Giver of the Revelation, more hope in the future of the world under his control, and a greater love for man, a broader philanthropy. The world would not outgrow it, but would forever grow by it; the highest consummations would find in it their fountains, and it should still be the crown and the glory of all.

If under the test of human experience these things are found to be true, then this word has shown itself to be altogether trustworthy, to be divine. Now we assert, without fear of successful contradiction, that the Bible has done, and is doing all this and more.

It reveals a thorough, accurate knowledge of man's nature and needs. There were no excuse for the Bible, if it were not to make man know himself and his possibilities as he could not otherwise know them. And it has given man such a conception of himself, of his dignity and destiny, as he had else never attained,—a conception which, when once it is gained, evidences its own truth.

Of whatever else man may be supposed to be ignorant, it would seem that he should be expected to know himself. He may be ignorant of the sun, and moon and stars, holding concerning them whatever crude and erroneous opinions he pleases; he may even misread the times and the seasons, and remain in primitive ignorance of the manifold forms of life about him in air, and earth, and sea. "Neither can he be expected to appreciate the vast and subtle harmonies at the outset of his career. He cannot be supposed to have mastered then the superb mechanism, the knowledge of which implies large inquiry, long experiment. The lightning for him will not have learned to run on his messages. The needle of the compass will not for him have become a seer, guiding his course amid the darkness, and loosing his keels from the visible headlands. * * And the

beautiful lights and the towering heights of philosophical speculation may long remain as unapproachable by him as rainbows cresting inaccessible summits. But one might suppose that man ought at once to know himself, in the very beginning of his manhood. The elements of that knowledge are within him. The faculty of that knowledge can hardly be expected to remain quiescent, until it is touched by some particular form of religious faith; but would at once awake to combine these elements of force," these promises of power, these institutions of an awakened soul into a knowledge of what he is, and what he may become; while at the same time he would recognize the best method of achieving from this actual the more glorious possible.

'Tis true that from the very beginning man did study man. He had inscribed over the door of his favorite temple in Greece the command, "Know thyself," long before the English poet wrote, "The proper study of mankind is man." Though the rolls of history are brilliant with the names of great and learned men, yet their philosophies had discovered but a little of what and whence man is. They so little understood man, that they had not learned half his dignity, or nobility of nature. Man received no consideration because he was a man. The impulse was to honor the accidents of power or station rather than the man. They worshipped the emperor as a God, but the slave, or soldier, or artisan was nothing save only as he might contribute to the comfort of the rich and powerful, as he might add to the glory of the State, or increase its prosperity. Man, it was thought, sprang from swamps, or rocks, or trees, or as the Sparti from the teeth of Dragons. The first men were only miserable animals dwelling in the caves of the mountains, or excavations in the earth. Then what is there in man as man, they asked, which is worthy of more consideration than is given to beasts? Only when he had power, or wealth, either by birth or acquisition was he worthy of regard. That there was a future life, some hoped, as did Socrates, and Cicero, and Plato; but Cæsar, the pontifex maximus as well as emperor, proclaimed publicly in the Senate, that there was no future life for men. The Brahman anticipated a future life, but it was only a repetition of the life which he saw about him, the life of an ox, or goat, or some insect, or reptile. He hoped that some time in the dim future he might chance once again to be born a man. But this was not in any modern sense an immortal life. Buddhism knew no God. Its future promised only an unconscious existence, such as the body might have after the soul has departed. Of the few enlightened ones it speaks with deference, but the mass of men it compares to "rubbish."

No wonder that among such people, though refined as were the Greeks, or powerful as were the Romans, or civilized as are the Hindus, women were only the servants of man's lust, not so much man's companion as his slave. No wonder that children were exposed to starvation, or as a prey to cruel and ravenous beasts; for woman was not powerful, and infancy was helpless.

It was to men striving thus to know, yet not knowing themselves, that the Bible came with revelations, which they have been compelled to acknowledge are true.

It taught man the dignity and worth of manhood. It revealed the fact that he was made in the image of a God, whom it taught him to know more perfectly. He was not all of the swamp, or of the earth, but there had been breathed into him a living rational soul. And man could not deny it, for the soul had evidenced its existence to him in every thought. He is taught that a divine being has formed him, and endowed him with powers and faculties like its own. Just as the impress of Cæsar's head upon the coin gave it a recognized worth throughout the world; so wherever the truth is accepted, that man is created in the image of God, it adds to manhood a new, dignity and demands for him a new respect.

All this is enhanced by the evident consideration which God accords to even the lowest man, the meanest slave. Does it not at once raise man in his own esteem to know that he is the object of such divine solicitude, that he is of such dignity as that God stoops to commune with him, and to show him the divine will? It takes heavenly truth and puts it to the service of man, because even heavenly truth is not too precious for his use. And then when he discovers that this revelation is given to all men, because they are men, and not to those only who are kings and priests, to the rich and the mighty of the earth; when it is found that there is one truth for all, one hope for all, one destiny possible for all, whether peasant or king, provided only that he accept and trust in the mercy of God; then man learns that there is a glory in his very manhood stripped of all the accidents of life. In this book "there is neither Greek nor Jew, there is neither bond nor free, there is neither male nor female, but all are one in Christ.'' And the astonished believer is led to exclaim, "what is man that thou art mindful of him ? and the son of man, that thou visitest him ? Thou hast made him a little lower than the angels, and hast crowned him with glory and honor.''

But this conception of man's worth in God's estimation is further materially elevated, when we behold Christ as God's gift for us. Whatever may have been thought of man before, since Christ has taken upon himself our nature, it has always and everywhere been exalted. None dare longer despise it. For He, who is all divine, has become in our behalf a perfect man, that in us might be realized the full possibilities of our humanity. But this is not all that we are taught of the dignity of our own nature in the incarnation. We see Christ not only living that we may be blessed, but dying in greatest ignominy, despised and rejected by his foes, deserted by his friends, suffering the curse of the cross, the power of death, the confinement of the tomb, that he might redeem man from the power of sin unto God. Now it matters not for the moment whether all this be true, or not. I am now claiming only, that this is the representation of the Bible. In it at least God has so highly valued man as man, that all, who have been brought under its sway, have learned to look upon him as possessed of a value, such as they had not else dreamed. For there must always "be a certain proportion between means employed and the ends desired; between benefits proffered and the accredited worth of the recipient. Even men do not build costly ships to carry sea-sand from Sidon to Ascalon,

and drop it into the deep; but only to carry wealthy fabrics, products of art, or treasures of looms, between the rich commercial cities. Even men do not send armed cohorts to conquer rabbits, or to capture mice.'' Therefore, if it be true as this book represents, that God sent his son into the world, to draw it into a new relationship to him by dying for it, then the immeasurable worth of the son of God, becomes the measure of the "greatness, in native constitution, in wealth of being of him for whom Christ came.''

It adds no little to the conception of man's dignity, which this book affords, that it recognizes and respects the freedom of the human will. Man is conscious, that he has the power of choice. Morality could not exist without it. The general may demand obedience of his soldiers even at the muzzle of the musket; or the master may exact obedience of his slave under the crack of the lash, but this Bible represents God as reasoning with man, as one would reason with his equal, or with the son whom he loved. "Come now, and let us reason together.'' The will of man is free; God made it so. God himself does not compel it, but appeals to it; he does not force it, but persuades it; he does not sway it by might, but by reason; he does not conquer it by power, but by love. He, therefore, gave man liberty to choose between good and evil. And it is just as true, that a man's destiny turns upon his own election, as it is that it turns upon the eternal election of God.

This is a high estimate to put upon man, simply as man. It was not conceived, except by these writers, who claim for themselves the inspiration of the Almighty.

And yet is it not true? The eye of the new born babe responds no more certainly to the light of the sun, nor the wing of the bird to he air, than does the consciousness of man to the truthfulness of this revelation of his dignity.

I ask you to notice also that the Bible not only affords what men are constrained to acknowledge is the only adequate conception of man's native worth, but that it also reveals its full acquaintance with his constitution. It recognizes all the parts and faculties of his being, the body, the mind and the spirit, with all their limitations and all their powers, and in their true subordination.

Of the body it shows, that there is no disregard of its preservation, even though it be enjoined to "keep it under." The cry of Christianity to those threatening to lay violent hands upon it is, "do thyself no harm." It tell us, that our "body is the temple of the Holy Ghost." When after death it is laid in the grave, over the open tomb its voice is heard saying, "It is sown a natural body, it is raised a spiritual body. It is sown in corruption, it is raised in incorruption." "I am the resurrection and the life."

It recognizes the intellect of man by setting before him a revelation which, while it is so simple that a child may understand from it what is necessary to please God, yet does not shirk any of the more difficult problems of life, with which it may be called to deal. It invites man to "grow in knowledge." It constantly appeals to him, as to one who can know and understand even the eternal things which it claims to reveal. The final problem of knowledge, which it proposes for his mind, is "to know him, whom to know aright is life eternal," and

it assures man, that at last he shall "know, even as he is known."

It moreover makes new demands upon his affections, yet with the certainty that they are not impossible. Love for the gods had never been possible under ethnic religions. The common people could not love their cruel deities. Their worship was paid in dread; it was the tribute of fear. The philosopher could not love the impersonal power, unembodied and infinite, which his reason had discerned, any more than a fish can love the cool breezes of summer, or the bird the stone which smote it. But this religion demanded of man a supreme love for its God, an affection "beside which all other affections should be weak, but from which they should take, each one, a higher purity, and a fresh consecration. Filial and fervent it was to be; persistent in energy, and of passionate intensity; such as could conquer pain and grief, outlast the years, survive vicissitudes, be only more mighty in the midst of temptations, be only supreme in the presence of death." And yet man's soul was capable of such a love as this, though it had never before been challenged or exhibited.

Other religions and systems of ethics had appealed for their authority either to man's fears, or to his innate selfishness. But this Bible appeals to him as a moral being, who has in himself a sense of right, a conscience demanding obedience, which men shall yield because it is right, in spite of the lusts of the body, or the passions of the soul. Its appeal to the conscience, that moral power in every man, was made through the affections and the intellect. It boldly declares God to be a spirit, and demands for him a spiritual worship.

It presents motives and reasons to the conscience through the intellect with the assurance that the intellect in man is capable of all this.

If now the Bible is indeed a revelation to man of his true dignity, if it has shown him, more clearly than he ever saw it before, the constitution of that organism of which it was said, "it is fearfully and wonderfully made," it no less clearly presents to his awakened soul possibilities, nay more, assurances of future privileges and attainments of which man had else caught only the faintest indication, or observed only the fading traces, as of dreams preserved in waking hours. But in the Bible "life and immortality are brought to light," and we may assure ourselves of them, as we do of the visions of the day. Where many had asked the question, "if a man die, shall he live again?" it was only here, that the answer was given with the assurance of certainty, "he that believeth on me, though he die, yet shall he live." For his future it presents a life, not like this baser, earthly life which Mohammed promised the faithful, but one of communion in thought and purpose with Almighty God, a life in which the soul, not the body, is guaranteed its highest enjoyments. He is promised through the redemption of Christ a participation in the divine nature, adoption into the family of God, and the ultimate attainment of true holiness. The command has gone forth, "Be ye holy, for I am holy," and to this holiness he is lead by all the operations of divine grace, and all the dealings of Providence.

If this were all that the Bible taught man, it would have failed to recognize one of his most conspicuous difficulties, and would have left him impotent to achieve the glorious possibilities which it displayed. But in the very midst of its revelations of man's marvelous endowments and opportunities, it raises a trumpet voice of warning and reproach for sin. By the greatness of his nature he is to measure the depth of his degredation in sin. It holds up to his view the weakness, the bondage, the destruction in which he stands, until it wrings from him the cry of anguish, "O wretched man that I am! Who shall deliver me from the body of this death?"

He would be a helpless and unhelping doctor, who though he could name all the muscles and bones, and organs of the human system, and though he could rightly diagnosis every case, if he could do no more, if he had no remedy, that could cure the disease, if he could give no relief to the suffering. And so of this book, if the Bible stopped here, and had no remedy for man's sin, no escape from its condemnation, no restoration to his primitive holiness, or nothing to make him better than it found him, then we should doubt whether it came from God. In this one thing in which man most needs help and a revelation from his Maker, the Ruler of the universe, it would disappoint all his expectations, and leave him to the bitterness of despair.

But the Bible is not thus helpless. For man's sin, it shows a fountain opened; it invites him with the assurance, that "though your sins be as scarlet, they shall be as white as snow; though they be red like crimson, they shall be as wool." Your penalty another, in the supreme sacrifice of love, has borne in your stead, and "there is now, therefore, no condemnation" to those who are in him. For the day of his weakness, it promises "my strength is made perfect in weakness. "My grace is sufficient for you." In the presence of temptation, it affords a sure victory. It invites man to "come boldly to the throne of grace, that he may obtain mercy, and find grace to help in time of need." In his perplexities; it assures him of a divine guidance: amid his sorrows it offers a divine comfort; in his associations with his fellows, it teaches principles of mutual respect and forbearance. It proclaims "liberty throughout the land unto all the inhabitants thereof;" it exalts nations in righteousness.

But we ask, are all these wonderful teachings true? Will they verify themselves in human experience? Do they meet the needs of man as an individual, and as a race? Or is it all only a beautiful picture, only a rainbow beauty, which may delight the eyes, but on which no man can climb up out of this sinful nature, and out of its sorrows into God's heaven of purity and love.

The answer is at hand. The test has been made by thousands, and the world throbs with a new life under the impulse of these truths. To use the words of another "it has not left the race as it found it. It is certain that no greater power ever entered the world. It has turned and overturned; it has grappled with and overthrown hoary superstition; it has eradicated huge and monstrous evils; it has ennobled manhood; it has elevated womanhood; it has thrown its protection around the helplessness of childhood; it has weakened the power of oppression; it has melted the chains of slavery; it has given sacredness to human life; it has imparted sanctity to marriage; it

has created the idea of a home; it has begotten the feeling of human brotherhood; it has diffused education and culture; it has elaborated by its preaching, and its worship, and its Sabbaths for divine uses, the noblest, the broadest, the purest types of human excellence that have ever appeared upon the earth. It needs only to contrast Christian with non-Christian communities to discover the benignity of its influences."

We have not claimed too much for this book, our enemies themselves being judges. Says the infidel Hume, in his history of England, in speaking of the results of the Saxon conquest, "they nearly extirpated the Christian religion, thereby causing the country to revert to its ancient barbarity." But the Bible was again sent to this barbaric nation, and its king, Ethelbert of Kent, was a little later baptized. The introduction into Briton for the second time of the gospel, the same historian tells us, was the "most memorable event in this reign." We know what these English speaking races now are, the foremost people of the world, in wealth, piety, enlightenment, and every right element of civilization and progress. The present Queen of Great Britain has herself sent in response to the question of an African chief for the secret of this greatness a Bible with the message, "This is the secret of England's greatness." Darwin, who would not take time to consider the claims of God upon him, yet seeing the results of the teaching of these truths in certain islands of the seas, became a regular contributor to the cause of foreign missions, saying, "The lesson of the missionary is that of the enchanter's wand." While Carlyle asserted with vehemence, "good never came from aught else."

Such testimony millions of people are ready to give to-day; other millions have lived in every age, who have experienced its truth, and who have testified, that in the Bible every need of man's spiritual nature is met; that all its promises are true; that its blessings give full content and joy; they have declared this, though the body was in nakedness and want, though it was racked with pains; they have confessed it in the arena, where they were placed to contend with wild beasts, because of their faith; and they have not denied it in the presence of fiercer man, by whom they were given to the rack, or brought to the martyr's stake. Is not their testimony true? Have they not experienced that of which they spake? Who are these people? They are the purest and the best. Their testimony would be taken in any court of equity as final. They come from all stations in life, and from all ages, and nations, and climes; they are men and women, whose faith has made the world brighter and better, and whose philanthropies have fallen upon the despised and the wretched as mercies from heaven.

With one voice, however, they ascribe it all to this book. They have made the experiment, and they say, that it is even as God's word declares.

But this is not all. The Bible invites you to make the experiment, and to know from your own experiences, whether these things are so or not. "Oh taste and see that the Lord is good." "If any man will do his will, he shall know of the doctrine whether it be of God." It challenges the test; it invites you to prove its truth; yea, it entreats your acceptance, and assures you, that just as you enter more and more fully into the life which it reveals, will you know,—for ye shall have the witness within yourselves —that in everything this Book is God's word, and worthy of all acceptation.

Will you make the experiment? "He that doeth his will, shall know of the doctrine whether it be of God."

The Effect of Modern Criticism upon the Trustworthiness of the Bible.

BY THE REV. WILLIAM P. SWARTZ.

✛ PART V. ✛

"PROVE ALL THINGS ; HOLD FAST THAT WHICH IS GOOD."
I Thess. v:21.

To criticise is to judge. Criticism, as a department of literature, is the science by which knowledge is tested as to its form, its truthfulness, its sufficiency. Its laws are the laws of probation. Its tendency and its purpose, when honest, are to separate the true from the false, that the true may be held and the false discarded. It is, as it were, the auditing of the accounts to see whether the books have been kept correctly, and whether their showing is trustworthy. It is the proving of the problem by such means as have been established for verifying the results of calculations. It tests the coin, which men are asked to receive in the commerce of thought, and determines whether it be gold or only a cheap alloy.

Honest criticism is, therefore, not merely permissible, it is demanded. "Prove all things; hold fast that which is good." In the renaissance of learning, when the awakening mind was confronted with great masses of tradition, of philosophy, of history so called, and of dogma, demanding acceptance and obedience, it began to ask, what of all this is truth, and what is error? The spirit of the unchained Bible was working in the liberated minds of the people, testing, reconstructing, and advancing all knowledge. The world had passed beyond the credulity of its childhood, when a legend was accepted as of equal authority, and, perhaps, of greater interest than history itself. It began, with the soberness of manhood, to demand such evidence for its acceptance and

faith, as the false could not give, but the true could readily furnish. It began to "prove all things." Under this scrutiny, much science was displaced by truer learning; much history was shown to be myth; and ancient philosophies ceased to be received as authority, and were studied chiefly as an indication of the attainments of the age in which they were produced. Nothing was accepted merely on the ground of venerable age, nothing on the strength of tradition only. The results of this sifting process have been very helpful to true advancement.

It is impossible that the Bible, which was more influential than any other book in inducing this spirit, should escape the scrutiny, which it demanded for everything else, and which it invited for itself. Some Christians in every age have manifested alarm for the safety of the Bible, and even of Christianity; and they have, therefore, sought to prevent the fullest criticism of its claims: they have shrunk for it from the knife and the glass. But the Bible itself has submitted fearlessly to the test, demanding of its critics only fair handling, and a readiness on their part to see and to acknowledge the truth.

It is foreign to the purpose of this paper to review the attacks of infidelity upon the cardinal doctrines of the word; such as the incarnation of Christ, the third person of the adorable Trinity; salvation through his perfect life and atoning death; a revelation to men in his life and word of the way back to

God and holiness; the eternity of its rewards and its punishments. These facts have not ceased to be assailed, it is true, but they have so frequently been vindicated, that it is only the wilfully ignorant, or the spiritually blind who any longer assail them. But there is a criticism, which, beginning at the time of the Reformation, has continued in varying forms, and with different objects in view to question the authority of the Bible, the correctness of its text, and the integrity and authenticity of its books. In short, it has taken up all the questions which present themselves concerning the Bible as literature, and which are preparatory to the use of the Bible for instruction and doctrine.

Let us examine briefly the scope and spirit of Modern Criticism, and its results as affecting the trustworthiness of the Bible.

There is, perhaps, nothing so commonly talked about, and of which people usually have so vague and confused ideas, as this one of Modern Biblical Criticism, especially of that department called the Higher Criticism.

There is placed in the hands of the critic a book, or rather a collection of books, commonly called the Bible; he is met with the assertion of the church, that this book is the Word of God, that it contains a literature different in its origin and purpose from all other literature; that it is not like the sacred books of any other religion, because they are human productions, but this, though written by men, was written by them only as they were moved by the Holy Ghost. The critic opens the book itself, and finds in a thousand places, and in many ways this claim repeated. Then arises the questions, "How shall I know that this claim is true? Why should these books, and none others, be included in this volume? What authority is there in the books themselves, or in history to support this claim?

1. These questions give rise to the first department of Biblical criticism, which is commonly called, the Criticism of the Canon, or Biblical Canonics.

The first answer given to the Reformers by the ecclesiastics was, "These are the Holy Scriptures, because the church says that they are." But Luther in his controversy with Eck said, "The church cannot give any more authority or power than it has of itself. A council cannot make that to be of scripture which is not by nature of scripture." Calvin says, "But there has very gener-

ally prevailed a most pernicious error, that the scriptures have only so much weight as is conceded to them by the church, as though the eternal and inviolable truth of God depended on the arbitrary will of men."

If the authority of the church could not in the days of the Reformation give canonicity to the books of the Bible, neither could it in any other age subsequent to the apostles; and there is no good evidence that the apostles ever did collect a canon of scripture. If these books had been accepted upon the decree of a council in any age, they would rest for their authority upon human judgment. This can certainly have no more acceptance with thinking minds, when it frames a canon of scripture, than when it frames any doctrine or dogma, as that of the papal infallibility, or penance, or of the mass.

How may I then know, that any writing is or is not of God's revealed word? The answer of Calvin and of all the Reformers with him was, "For, as God alone is a sufficient witness of himself in his own Word, so also the Word will never gain credit in the hearts of men, till it is confirmed by the internal testimony of the Spirit. It is necessary, therefore, that the same Spirit, who spake by the mouths of the prophets, should penetrate into our hearts, to convince us that they faithfully delivered the oracles which were divinely entrusted to them." The great test, therefore, of the divinity of any writing is the Holy Spirit in it evidencing its inspiration. The testimony of Christians in all past ages was not rejected as worthless, nor the voice of the church as of no confirming power; but it was rightly demanded, that if any writing is of divine authority, it must manifest that authority to the heart and mind of the devout reader now as well as in the past. "The evangelical test of canonicity and inspiration of the Scriptures was, God Himself speaking in and through them to His people. This alone gave the fides divina. This was the so-called formal principle of the Reformation."

Now this test was applied to each book for which the Roman Catholic church demanded acceptance, and as a result the apocryphal books were rejected from the canon. Did the position of the critic in the Reformation weaken the truth, or impair the hold which it had upon the world? It made the canon narrower, but it strengthened the power of that which was left. Says one of the most pronounced of our modern evangelical workers in the field of Biblical criticism, "We believe that the canon of Scriptures established by the Reformed symbols can be successfully vindicated on Protestant critical principles. We believe, that the church has not been deceived with regard to its inspiration."

No man is, therefore, called upon to receive this book as God's word, because the church says that it is, or because of its antiquity only, but because all through the ages, to multitudes of prayerful readers, and to multitudes in this age it is evidencing its divinity by the power of its truth, and the accompanying work of the Holy Ghost in man; and because it will prove itself to you, if you will put it to the test. But what has been the effect of this position upon the trustworthiness of the word? It has removed its claim for acceptance from a false to a true foundation, where it can much better evidence its unfailing trustworthiness.

2. But when once the canonicity and authority of the books were established, critics asked, have we the text as it was written? In seeking the answer they gathered the different manuscripts and versions, ransacking every library in cathedral, and university, and monastery. These manuscripts were then carefully examined to discover which was the oldest, for it would probably be the nearest to the original as it left the hand of its human author. Then every manuscript, which could be found, was compared with it, verse by verse, word by word, letter by letter, until every variation in the reading of all the manuscripts was noted and catalogued. After that each different reading was taken up, and by the weight of evidence for or against it, it was accepted or rejected. At last one text resulted, or practically one, under the hand of different critics, working with all the material that they could find, in different countries, and by independent judgment. It is from this text that our revised version of the Bible has been translated. This department of criticism is called the Textual, or Lower Criticism.

At first infidels made much of the great number of different readings which had been found, 150,000 in the New Testament. They asserted, that whatever might be claimed for the Bible as it was first composed, it must be allowed, that the Bible which exists is neither infallible, nor inspired; for behold, say they, how it differs in one manuscript from another. But the analysis of the critics speedily dispelled the alarm. For of these readings perhaps nineteen-twentieths are of no authority, no one can suppose them to be genuine. Of the remainder nineteen-twentieths do not in the least affect the sense; and of the rest, not one of them touches any doctrine which the church has commonly taught. Dr. Scrivener, the author of what competent judges pronounce the best work in the English language on the Criticism of the Text of the New Testament, quotes from Bently, whom he calls "at once the profoundest and the most daring of English critics," the following emphatic testimony: "Make your variations as many more, and put them into the hands of a knave or a fool, and yet with the most sinister and absurd choice, he shall not extinguish the light of any one chapter, nor so disguise Christianity, but that every feature of it shall still be the same." "Thus," adds Dr. Scrivener, "hath God's providence kept from harm the treasure of his written Word, so far as is needful for the quiet assurance of His Church and people." To quote Dr. Briggs, "Such criticism has accomplished great things for the New Testament text. It will do even more for the Old Testament. * * * [Criticism] disturbs the inspiration of versions, the inspiration of the Massoretic text, the inspiration of particular letters, syllables, and external words and expressions; and truly all those who rest on these external things ought to be disturbed and driven from the letter to the spirit, from clinging to the outer wall, to see him who is the sum and the substance, the Master and the King of the Scriptures." [Biblical Study p. 162.] In all this scholars were merely applying to the Bible, with infinite advantage to the faith of Christendom, its own injunction, "Prove all things; hold fast that which is good."

3. Now the Bible had to pass to the test of a third form of criticism. For having determined that these books are God's inspired word, that they are canonical, and having recovered what must be very approximately the original text, there remained other tasks to demand the critic's skill, and patience,— tasks more difficult than either of those which he had successfully accomplished. Taking the text as thus secured, criticism must next consider it as literature, upon the same principles upon which other literature is examined. It asks concerning its authorship, its integrity,

its authenticity, and the circumstances as far as they can be learned under which it was produced. These are important questions, and help, as they are answered, to a better understanding of the sacred word. This is the Higher Criticism, in contradistinction to the criticism of the text, which is called the Lower Criticism. Now the Higher Criticism employs all facts, which it is able to gather from history, but it relies chiefly upon the evidence gathered from the writings themselves for the answer which it seeks. It examines as with a microscope the language of each part of the different books, noticing the style, the use or the neglect of certain distinctive forms of expression; it carefully notes all archæological references; it considers the historical allusions; and then it ascends to the thoughts of the author respecting the various branches of human knowledge and seeks the circumstances out of which they issue.

One of its chief maxims, as indeed a maxim of all criticism is, that nothing can be relied upon as really known, until it has been tested and found reliable by criticism. It is evident, therefore, that criticism itself needs the correction of criticism. It must again and again correct its processes and verify its results. It is well, therefore, to accept the results of criticism slowly, allowing ample time for the repeated verification to be made. In the mean time do not be alarmed at its announcements, many of which have already yielded and others will still yield to further criticism. For if as many errors had been found in the Bible as have been demonstrated to exist in the results of criticism of the Bible, it would be hard to maintain its authority as God's word. But criticism is man's best attempt to obey the command, "Prove all things; hold fast that which is good," and while he has had to acknowledge many mistakes, he has still brought to the surface with the dirt many rich gems of truth.

On this field of Higher Criticism there are entered three classes of workers. First are the scholastic critics, who have taken up the work to show that the traditional views taught in the schools are true. Next are the rationalistic often called the negative critics, whose purpose is to show that the Bible and hence Christianity, is only an evolution of human progress, requiring no divine interposition and giving no evidence of any. Of this school were Welhausen and Kennen, and Strauss, and Robertson Smith. As a third class there are Christian men who have felt the power of God in his word. These simply seek the truth concerning this word, assured that though it may overthrow accepted views, it will only promote the glory of God, and make it easier for men to defend the truth, and to discern the power of God's working among the nations in all ages.

Even as the discovery of the truth, now so firmly established, that our system is not earth-centered but sun-centered, has shown a greater power and wisdom in that Creator, and promoted his glory as the light of truth has flashed from furthest stars upon the wondering worshiper. The only ones injured by truth are those scientists and ecclesiastics, who lived like spiders in the tangled web of error spun from their own inner-consciousness. When these cob-webs of error were swept away to let in the light of God's truth, of course the spiders were in alarm as though all were destroyed. But afterward it is lighter.

The Higher criticism is, therefore, a great system of warfare, in which the same weapons may be used, according to the same canons of criticism, but with which there is being fought out on the field of the Bible the old warfare between the true and the false, between faith and infidelity. We are of course interested in the contest, but are not doubtful of the result, for God's word is truth, and it will prevail.

Already a number of battles of this warfare have been fought, and in every instance the rationalistic critics have been vanquished. Shall we not therefore, glory in these triumphs? Of the results of the battle in the age of the Reformation, let me quote the words of Dr. Draper in his Intellectual Development of Europe, a work which has never been charged with partiality toward the Bible. He says: "If criticism, thus standing on the basis of the Holy Scriptures, had not hesitated to apply itself to an examination of the public faith, and as a consequence thereof had laid down new rules for morality and the guidance of life, it was not to be expected, that it would hesitate to deal with minor things, that it would spare the philosophy, the policy, the literature of antiquity. And so, indeed, it went on, comparing classical authors with classical authors, the fathers with the fathers, often the same writer with himself. Contradictions were pointed out, errors exposed, weaknesses detected, and new views offered of almost everything in the range of literature. From this burning ordeal one book alone came out unscathed. It was the Bible. It spontaneously vindicated for itself, what Wiclif in the former times, and Luther more lately, had claimed for it. And not only did it hold its ground, but it truly became incalculably more powerful than ever it had been before." [Draper's Intellectual Development of Europe, vol. II, p. 224.]

The battle for the historical character and date of the Gospels has been fought out, and the negative critics have been put to flight. In the second paper of this series reference was made to the mythical theory of Strauss, and to the support which it received from the Tuebingen school of critics, with Bauer at their head, in claiming that the Gospels were not histories, but the late records of myths which had arisen in the first and second centuries concerning Jesus. None of the Gospels, it was asserted, were written in the Apostolic age, but in the second century; and especially of the Gospel of John was it true, that it could not have been written until the second half of the second century, A. D. 160 to 170. The Evangelical party of the higher critics began to search the literature of antiquity for its testimony to the age of this Gospel. The Clementine Homilies, written about the time which Bauer said was the earliest date for the Gospel of John contained, this critic claimed no reference to this Gospel nor quotation from it. But only a part of these Homilies was extant. In 1853 a German scholar found a complete copy of the Homilies in the original, and published it. Now the complete Homilies contain undeniable quotations from the Gospel of John, which these critics said, had not yet been written. But they had to acknowledge their error, though not yet willing to accord the Gospel apostolic origin, or authenticity. But another witness was soon to be called against them. It had long been known that Tatian the Syrian, who died somewhere about 150 or 170 A. D. had written a work called the Diatesseron, supposed to be a harmony of the four Gospels. But the rationalistic critics said, "There is no authority for saying that Tatian's Gospel is a harmony of the four Gospels at all." "No one seems to

have seen the Tatian's Harmony for the very good reason that there was no such work." And again, "It is obvious that there is no evidence whatever connecting Tatian's Gospel with those of our canon." [See Supernatural Religion, Vol. II, p. 152 ff.] But the Diatesseron has been found. And is one Gospel made by weaving the accepted texts of the four canonical Gospels into one, using the text of John as the basis. This was a most disastrous blow to the rationalists, for it shows that in the time of Tatian and of his Master, Justin Martyr, [A. D. 103 to A. D. 169,] all the Gospels were not only in existence, but had obtained recognition and acceptance. One more witness was to overwhelm and rout those who were thus already seeking a safe way for retreat. In the work of Hypollitus, the Refutation of all Heresies, the author in dealing with the Heresy of Basilides, who flourished about 125 A. D., quotes a passage from Basilides as follows: "And this," he, [Basilides], says, "is that which has been stated in the Gospels: "He was the true light which lighteth every man that cometh into the world." So it had to be acknowledged that before the year 125 A. D. the Gospels, and particularly the Gospel of John were both written and generally accepted as of authority. Thus was the battle fought out concerning each of the Gospels by the higher critics, and there is now no doubt that the Gospels were all written in the time of the Apostles. Bauer assigned dates for the composition of these four Gospels which aggregated 605 years; but if the dates assigned by the last of the rationalistic critics of this school be added they make only 348 years. So the retreat on the ages of the four Gospels has been about 250 years.

Dr. Briggs says in his Biblical Study: "There has nothing been established by modern critical work, that will at all disturb the statements of the symbols of the Reformation with reference to the authority of the word of God."

On the other hand we may note some additional gratifying achievements of the Higher Criticism.

"The higher criticism has been compelled by rationalists and deists to meet the question of the forgery of the biblical writings. This phase of the subject has now been settled so far that no reputable critics venture to write of any of our canonical writings as forgeries." [Briggs Biblical Study, p. 222.]
We have not troubled ourselves to

mention the questions which are not yet settled,—such as the Mosaic Authorship of the Penteteuch, or the integrity of Isaiah, or the dates of the historical books. Concerning these questions final results have not yet been obtained. When once the divine authorship is established for any writing by the test which the Reformers proposed, and upon which all of our canon rests, and must rest; it matters not so much who wrote any particular part of the word, it is still God's word. When I recognize the signature of God, can I be shaken in my trust of his revelation, if it be found that another pen than that which I had supposed was employed by him in giving me this message? Rest assured, that the word which has successfully stood so many tests, and has vindicated its right to be called the Word of God, will never be found contradicting the truth.

In summing up, therefore, the results of the Higher Criticism upon the trustworthiness of the Bible, I cannot do better than to quote again the words of Dr. Briggs: "The higher criticism has already strengthened the credibility of the Scriptures. It has studied the human features of the Bible, and learned the wondrous variety of form and color assumed by the divine revelation. Many of the supposed inconsistencies have been found to be different modes of representing the same thing, complementary to one another and combining to give a fuller representation than any one mode ever could have given; as the two sides of the stereoscopic view give a representation superior to that of the ordinary photograph. Many of the supposed inconsistencies have been found to arise from different stages of the divine revelation, in the earlier of which God condescended to the ignorance and weakness of men, and gave to them the knowledge which they could appropriate, and held up to them ideals which they could understand as to their essence if not in all their details. The earlier are shadows and types, crude and imperfect representations of better things to follow. Many of the supposed inconsistencies resulted from the popular and unscientific language of the Bible, thus approaching the people of God in different ages in concrete forms and avoiding the abstract. Many of the inconsistencies have resulted from the scholastic abstractions of those who would use the Bible as a text book, but they do not exist in the concrete of the Bible itself. Many of the supposed inconsistencies arise from a different method of logic and rhetoric in the Oriental writers, and the attempt of modern scholars to measure them by Occidental methods. Many of the inconsistencies result from the neglect to appreciate the poetic and imaginative element in the Bible and a lack of æsthetic sense on the part of its interpreters. The higher criticism has already removed a large number of these difficulties, and will remove many more as it becomes a more common study among scholars." These are the words of Dr. Briggs, one of the critics. We have now answered the question before us and with grateful hearts we may acknowledge, and accept this precious book, from which we have received so many lessons for this life, from which we have found so much comfort in the hours of our bereavement, which has given so much of divine grace in the time of trial, which has done so much to better our own life and to enlighten and bless the world—we may rest upon this book as the Word of God, eternal truth. For it has stood the test of harmony with the latest reading of God's other book, the volume of nature, and it is the only book of antiquity which has stood this test. It has often been challenged and contradicted by historians, but it has always maintained its correctness, and they have been proved in error. It has been assailed upon the ground of its unfulfilled prophecy, but the critical study of the prophecies has more than any other thing declared the books divine. And again it has demonstrated its divinity in the experience of multitudes, who have "done God's will," and have thus learned that the word is His. And now we have seen that all the attacks of its enemies have but served to enhance its authority and to increase its power that in no single point has its trustworthiness been weakened by the results of criticism. No book has ever been so criticised, and none has proved itself of like quality; for all others have been shown to be only man's work, but this is the work of God.

As this book is then so firmly proven to be God's revelation to you, take it as the authority of your life, trust it implicitly, submit to it in all things, and it will sanctify you, and keep you for that greater glory which is still to be revealed, when He who is the Living Word shall appear.